Green Kids

SAVING WATER

SAVING ENERGY

RECYCLING

Neil Morris

JN/2230279

Consultant: Terry Jennings
Project Editor: Anya Wilson
Design and Picture Research: Dynamo Design

Copyright © QED Publishing 2010

First published in the UK in 2010 by
QED Publishing
A Quarto Group Company
226 City Road a
London EC1V 2TT

www.qed-publishing.co.uk

ISBN 978 1 84835 415 9

Printed in China

The words in **bold** are
explained in the Glossary
on page 116.

Contents

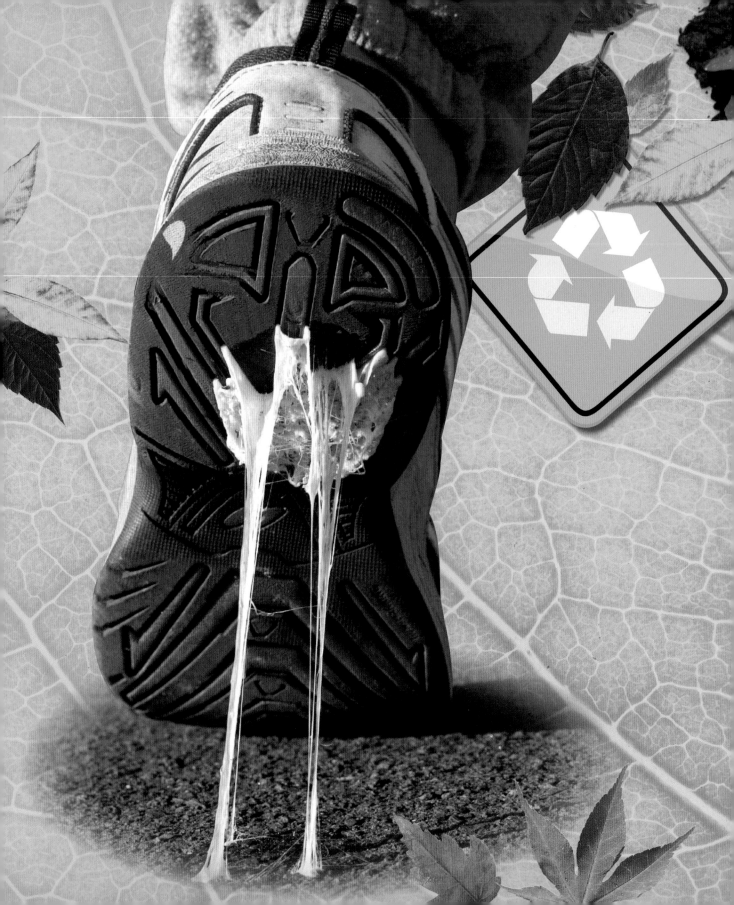

Looking after my environment

Learn all about how you can help to protect the environment. Why not organize a litter clean-up at school? Or plant some seeds to make your garden greener? Make caring for the world around you fun as well as helpful.

Green ideas

The **environment** is the world around us. It includes the land, air and sea. Green ideas can help us to look after our surroundings. Being 'green' means caring for the environment.

You can do it

You can help the environment by starting a 'Green Club'. Invite your family and friends to join. Use ideas from this book and add some of your own.

You probably spend most of your time at home, in school and around your neighbourhood. This is your own special environment. It is up to you to look after it and make sure it is not spoiled.

▲ *We can all enjoy our neighbourhood more if we keep it clean.*

No litterbugs!

▲ *Litterbugs make extra work for street cleaners.*

Litter is pieces of rubbish left on the ground. It spoils the environment because a lot of it is not **biodegradable**, which means that it will never rot away. You can help by making sure you are never a **litterbug**.

Did you know?

In most countries, it is illegal to throw litter on the ground. Litterbugs can be made to pay a fine.

Litter can be as small as a sweet wrapper or an old piece of chewing gum – which is very annoying when it gets stuck to your shoe! Litterbugs are thoughtless because it is easy to use a rubbish bin, or keep things until you get home.

◄ Old chewing gum should be wrapped and put in a rubbish bin. It is not biodegradable, so it will stay on the ground forever!

9

Cleaning up

▲ Some people believe that graffiti is street art, but others think it is deliberate damage.

When spray paints are used to draw or write on walls in the street, it is called graffiti. **Local councils** usually scrub graffiti off walls, but this costs time and money.

You can do it!

Ask an adult to help you to organize a litter clean-up at home or at school. You could **recycle** bottles, paper and cans.

No one likes to get dog's mess on their shoes. In many countries, it is against the law to let your dog foul in a public place. Dog owners should always clean up after their dog to keep public places clean.

◄ Dog owners should be responsible and carry a bag and scoop to clean up after their dog if they need to.

Too noisy!

Near an airport or on a busy street, it is often very noisy. If the noise is too loud, it can make people unhappy because it disturbs their everyday life. This is called noise **pollution**.

Did you know?

Noise is measured in decibels. Normal conversation is about 50 decibels, loud music is about 80 decibels and a jet engine is 120 decibels.

◀ When planes take off and land, they make a lot of noise. People who work near airport runways wear ear protection so their hearing is not damaged.

We all make noise in our daily lives, but we should try to think of others. When we are outdoors, we can turn down the radio, talk quietly rather than shout and generally make less noise.

▲ We can still have fun if we talk quietly with our friends!

Fresh air

◀ We need to breathe fresh air to be healthy. There are often fewer cars in the countryside, so there is less pollution.

We breathe in oxygen gas from the air around us. All living things need this gas to live and grow. It is important that the air is clean, so we do not breathe in harmful gases.

The air can become dirty, even though we cannot see it. When people burn **fuels** to drive cars and make things in factories, waste gases are given off.

The greenhouse effect is where waste gases act like the glass in a greenhouse. The gases can come from burning fuels, such as petrol in a car. They trap the Sun's heat and this is slowly heating up the Earth. This process is called global warming.

▲ Waste gases stay in the Earth's atmosphere and stop heat from escaping. This is called the greenhouse effect.

Walking and cycling

We can help the environment by walking or cycling short distances, instead of riding in a car or bus.

Then we will not burn fuels such as petrol, so we do less harm to the environment.

▶ *Walking to school is fun and good for you. It also helps the environment by saving energy.*

Do you have lots of safe walking and cycling routes near your home and your school? Good pavements, pedestrian crossings and cycle lanes make it easier for us to get about without polluting the air.

▲ When you ride a bike, your muscles provide all the energy you need.

You can do it!

You and your friends could use a 'walking school bus'. You need an adult driver and conductor to lead you safely to school.

On holiday

On holiday, people often visit beaches and beauty spots. Picnic areas in the countryside are popular, too. These places can easily become littered because so many people visit them.

▲ A picnic is great fun. It is important not to leave any litter behind.

You can do it!

Next time you are on the beach or having a picnic in the park, count the pieces of litter lying around. Which items make up most of the litter?

▲ *Birds' feathers can become clogged with oil from spills at sea. Wildlife protection agencies try to clean as many birds as possible.*

The coast and seaside are especially at risk. Big ships can pollute the shore with oil spills and the beaches become littered. In some places, **sewage** is pumped into the sea, too.

Tree power

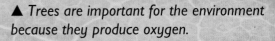

Plants give off oxygen gas that we need to breathe. They also take in a gas called carbon dioxide, which we breathe out. This is why the largest plants — trees — are such an important part of the environment.

▲ *Trees are important for the environment because they produce oxygen.*

You can do it!

Ask for permission to plant some apple and orange pips, plum stones or conkers in your garden or school grounds. You could grow a new tree and help the environment.

▲ We need to plant more trees to replace all those that we cut down.

The wood from trees is used to make things, including paper. We use so much wood that more trees are being cut down than are being planted. Are there plenty of trees in your local park? And are there some in your street?

All together

There are lots of ways to look after our environment. We can stop littering, save energy and use less water. We can also help to **reduce** pollution, keep our neighbourhood clean and recycle goods.

Did you know?

The cigarette butt is the biggest litter item in the world. About 4.5 billion of them are dropped in the street every year. Next come sweet wrappers and drinks cans.

▲ We can all help by taking waste to paper and bottle banks. It is much better than throwing things away.

These are green ideas, and they are all worth doing. If every one of us tries hard to do something to look after the environment, our small actions will add up to big results.

Recycling

Find out all the facts that will help you to reduce, reuse and recycle. Why not start up a 'swap shop' with your friends? Or try using cloth bags instead of plastic ones? Get to grips with recycling!

That's rubbish!

Rubbish is made up of things that we throw away because we do not want them any more. It is also called waste. An empty drinks bottle is rubbish because the drink has been drunk.

Did you know?

In rich countries, each person throws away a sack of rubbish every ten days — a village of 350 people would produce an elephant's weight in waste every week!

We throw all kinds of things away. Our waste includes paper and card, glass bottles, metals and plastic. Kitchen and garden waste, and old clothes and rags are also thrown away.

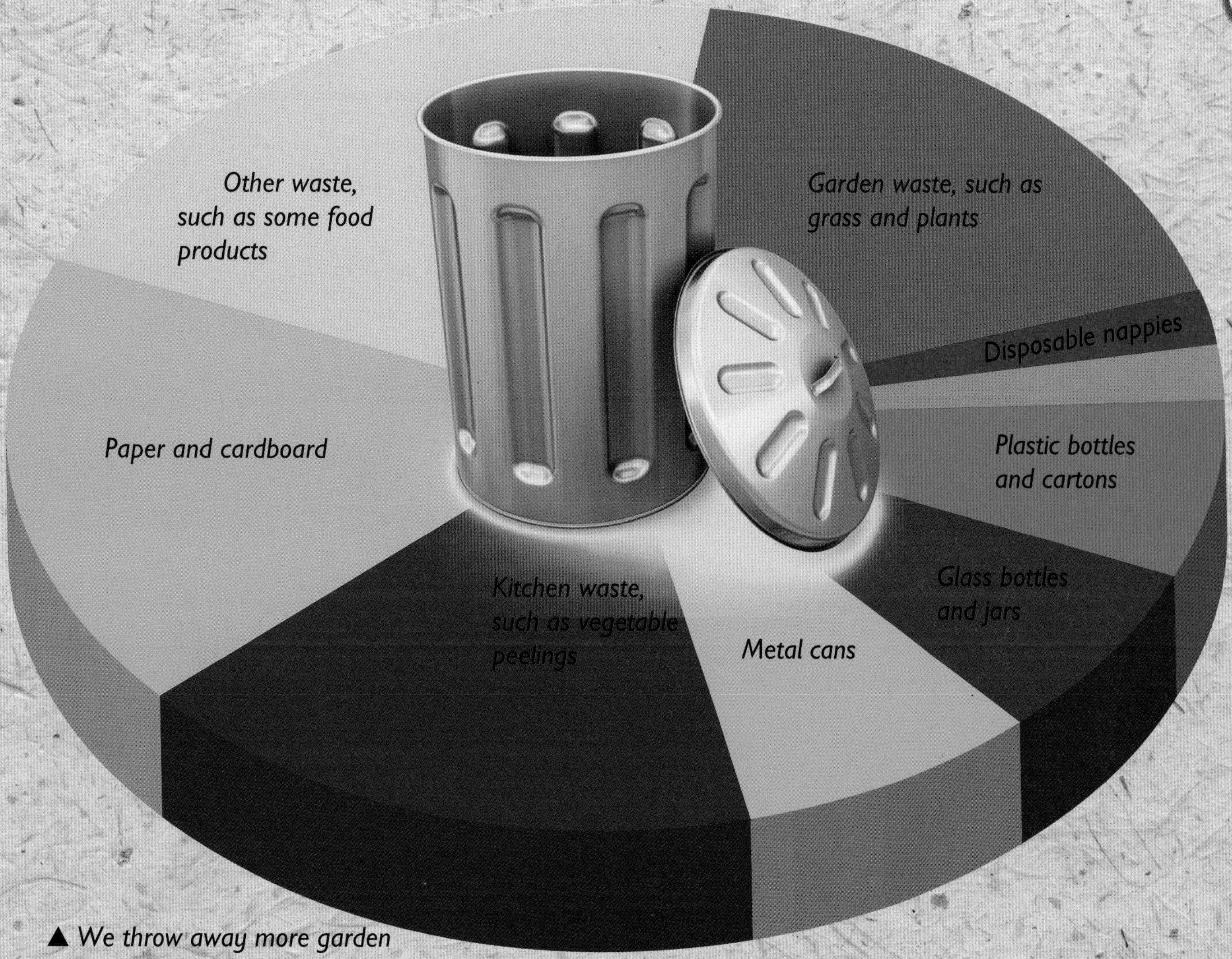

Other waste, such as some food products

Garden waste, such as grass and plants

Disposable nappies

Paper and cardboard

Plastic bottles and cartons

Glass bottles and jars

Kitchen waste, such as vegetable peelings

Metal cans

▲ We throw away more garden waste and paper than any other product. Most of the things shown here can be recycled, which would help the environment.

What happens to our waste?

General waste goes into bins and these are emptied into special lorries. The lorries collect waste from homes and schools.

▶ Rubbish lorries have machinery inside that crushes waste to make it smaller.

Rubbish lorries take most waste to **landfill sites.** There, the waste is tipped into a big hole in the ground. When the hole is full, the waste is buried.

▶ This landfill waste will eventually be covered with dirt. The land may then be used as a country park or a golf course.

The waste that is put into landfill sites in one minute would fill 15 buses.

▲ *Before waste is put into an incinerator and burned, large claws turn it over to dry it.*

Some of our waste is burned in large furnaces, which are hot ovens called **incinerators**.

29

The three Rs

We can help to produce less waste by putting the three Rs into action. The letters stand for reduce, **reuse** and recycle.

Reducing means cutting down on waste by using less in the first place. For example, we could use less **packaging**. Some foods are wrapped in plastic, but instead we could buy them without the packaging.

You can do it!

Start a 'swap shop' with your friends. Bring toys or books that you no longer use or need. Friends might like to swap them for something you want.

We can use things again instead of throwing them away. You could use a shoebox to store special toys or drawings.

▶ *Instead of being thrown away or recycled, a jam jar can be reused as a pen or pencil holder.*

Don't throw it away

When we throw things away, we waste the **materials** they are made from. It is better to recycle. Recycling makes a new product out of something that has been used before. For example, the glass in an old bottle can be used to make a new one.

▲ Empty plastic bottles and other containers can be recycled to make new ones.

When you go shopping, you can buy goods that have been recycled. Look out for the symbols or words that tell you notepads, tissues or toilet paper are made of recycled paper.

You can do it!

You could sort rubbish at home into groups, such as paper and cardboard, glass, metal and plastic. Find out where you can take the rubbish or when it is collected.

New paper for old

Trees are turned into **pulp**, which is then used to make paper. It takes a lot of energy to turn wood into paper. We can save trees and energy by using pulp from recycled paper.

▶ Trees are mashed into pulp, which will be used to make large sheets of paper. The sheets will then be cut to smaller sizes.

Did you know?

Making one tonne of recycled paper saves 17 trees. This makes 700 phone books and saves enough energy to heat your home for a year.

When paper from books and newspapers is recycled, the ink must be removed. Soap is added to the pulp to wash the ink away. Some recycled paper is not as bright white as non-recycled paper.

Recycled paper

◀ Normally, recycled paper is not **bleached**, so it may not be as white as bleached paper. This saves more energy and **chemicals**.

Non-recycled paper

Saving glass

Glass bottles and jars can be recycled many times. At the recycling plant, they are crushed. Then the glass is heated, so that it melts and can be shaped into new bottles.

You can do it!

Keep a chart of the glass bottles you recycle. Recycling one glass bottle saves enough energy to power ten energy-saving light bulbs for an hour.

There are three bottle banks for different-coloured glass. The colours – green, brown and clear – are separated because if they were mixed, the recycled bottles would be a dull, muddy colour.

▲ Bottle banks can be found in many places, including supermarkets, country parks and on main streets.

Different metals

Cans can be recycled, too. Most drinks cans are made of **aluminium** and food cans are **steel**. The cans are separated when they are recycled so the different metals do not mix together.

▲ Cans should be washed out before they are recycled. Food cans should also have their labels removed.

There is a simple way to tell steel from aluminium. Hold a magnet against the can. If the magnet sticks to the can, it is probably made of steel. Aluminium is not magnetic.

Old metal cans are made into new ones in the same way as glass. The cans are crushed, melted and reshaped.

◄ These drinks cans have been crushed together, ready to be melted down to make new cans.

You can do it!

Have an empty drinks can drive at school — see how many you can collect. Recycling one can saves enough energy to run a television for three hours.

Plastic problems

Plastic is a strong, light material made from oil. The world is running out of oil, so we need to recycle as much plastic as possible, or use other materials.

Did you know?

It takes three times more energy to make a new plastic bottle than a recycled one. Recycling one bottle saves enough energy to power a light bulb for six hours.

We can all help the environment by using fewer plastic bags. Materials that last a long time, such as fabric, are much better. Keep any plastic bags you are given, so that you can reuse them.

▲ Fabric bags or reusable bags made from recycled materials are better for the environment. Many supermarkets now provide them.

Green waste

Green waste comes from plants. It includes grass and leaves from the garden. Some green waste is made up of food leftovers, such as fruit and vegetable scraps.

▶ In autumn, leaves fall off the trees. They can be raked up and put in special green waste or compost bins.

Did you know?

Every year, each person throws away a huge amount of green waste - the same as almost 1000 banana skins. In landfill sites, green waste produces methane gas, which is very smelly!

Green waste can be recycled at home by making a compost heap or putting it into a compost bin.

▲ Compost looks like crumbly soil. It is made from green waste.

Over several months, the plants rot, making a crumbly material called compost. Gardeners use compost to grow new plants in because it is full of goodness.

43

Saving Water

Discover everything you need to know about how you can save water. Why not keep a rain diary of weekly rainfall? Or clean the family car with a bucket rather than a hosepipe? Saving water is fun!

Water everywhere

Water is all around us. It covers nearly three-quarters of our planet. The world's oceans, lakes and rivers are full of water. A lot of it is salty, which means we cannot drink it.

Did you know?

Water is inside every one of us, as well as all around us. Two-thirds of our body is made of water — including the brain, muscles, skin and blood.

All living things need water to live. We must drink lots of **fresh water** every day to stay healthy. Water is very valuable to us. It is important to use it wisely and save as much as we can.

▼A lot of water can be saved if you water plants using a watering can, rather than a garden hose.

Where does water come from?

Water comes from rain and it moves in a never-ending cycle. The water cycle is the journey water takes when it leaves the Earth's surface, goes into the sky and then returns to the Earth's surface.

The Water Cycle
1. Rain falls from clouds in the sky.
2. It flows to the sea in streams and rivers.
3. Heat from the Sun changes some of the liquid water into a gas called water vapour. The water vapour rises and makes more clouds.
4. Then the cycle starts again.

Fresh water is pumped to our homes, schools, offices and shops through large underground pipes. We just have to turn on the tap to get water!

▲ Large water pipes called **mains** are laid and buried underground.

Friday

Wednesday

Tuesday

Monday

You can do it!

You can see how much rain falls by leaving an empty pot, such as a jam jar, outside. Mark on the glass how much rain falls each day, and keep a weekly rain diary.

49

Drinking water

▼ *Water is cleaned in these tanks at a treatment works.*

Some people get water from **springs** and **wells**. Drinking water comes from **reservoirs**. To make it safe to drink, the water is cleaned at a treatment works.

Did you know?

It is impossible to think of a drink without water! Tea and coffee are made with hot water. There is water in squashes and fizzy drinks, too.

Some people buy sparkling or still water in bottles. If clean water is available from a tap, then bottled water is a waste of energy. This is because it takes extra energy to make the bottles and fill, label and transport them to shops.

▼ *Supermarkets sell many different brands of bottled water, from different springs around the world.*

All sorts of uses

▲ We need water to clean dirty dishes. We can save water by not letting the tap run.

Water is also used for washing, cooking, cleaning clothes and flushing the toilet. This adds up to an enormous amount of water, so we should only use as much as we need.

Some people use huge amounts of water without thinking. A garden sprinkler, for example, can use 600 litres of water in an hour. That is a bathful every eight minutes!

You can do it!

How much water does your family use in a week?

- Washing machine load — 60 litres
- Bath — 80 litres
- Shower — 30 litres
- Toilet flush — 10 litres

Turn off the tap!

Lots of clean water is wasted down the plughole of the bathroom or kitchen sink. The water flows through drains into large underground pipes, called **sewers**.

▲ *This waste water is flowing straight back into a river.*

There is an easy way to save water. When you are washing things, do not let the water run any longer than it has to. Use just the water you need and then turn off the tap.

You can do it!

Just for once, leave the cold tap running when you brush your teeth. If you leave the plug in, you can see how much water you've wasted. You'll be amazed!

Drip, drip, drip

Water is also wasted if taps do not work properly. A dripping tap might seem unimportant, but it could waste up to 25 litres of water a day.

▲ A plumber fixes water pipes if they have a leak.

Did you know?

Water companies repair pipes all the time, but there are still big leaks. Most companies lose at least one-tenth of their water through broken pipes.

Many modern washing machines and dishwashers use less water than older models.

They also save energy. We can save even more by only running them when they are full.

▲ *A washing machine that is only half full wastes water and energy.*

Collecting and recycling

We can reuse water on plants in the garden. The waste water left after washing vegetables or water from showers, kitchen sinks and washing machines is called 'grey water'. It is not drinkable, but it can be reused.

Rainwater can be collected and used to water plants. The easiest way is to use a barrel called a water butt. It gathers water from a drainpipe.

▶ *A water butt can store water during winter when it rains a lot. This can then be used in summer to water plants when there is little rain.*

Did you know?

If you clean the family car with water in buckets, you might use 30 litres. Using a hosepipe would use six times as much!

Dirty water

Some farmers spray chemicals on their crops to help them to grow and to protect them from pests. These chemicals can pollute underground water and nearby water sources, such as rivers.

Did you know?

More than one billion people in the world live without clean water — that's one in every six people.

Factories produce chemicals that can pollute rivers. Waste gases from cars and factories are also a problem. They mix with water in clouds to make **acid rain**. When acid rain falls, it can pollute lakes, kill trees and harm wildlife.

▼ *These trees have been damaged by acid rain.*

Around the world

In rich countries of the world, most people use about 200 litres of clean water each day. In poorer regions, water is much more precious – people only have 10 to 20 litres each

▲ *A reservoir is a large store of clean, fresh water.*

You can do it!

Make a poster to help people understand why it is important to save water and what they can do to help.

▲ *Some villages do not have clean running water, so people walk many kilometres to find water.*

In parts of Africa, there is often very little rainfall. This can cause a **drought** and the ground dries up. People get clean drinking water from a well. Dirty drinking water can make people very ill.

Saving Energy

Learn all about how you can save energy around your home and at school. Why not try using energy-saving light bulbs for a start? Saving energy is easy!

What is energy?

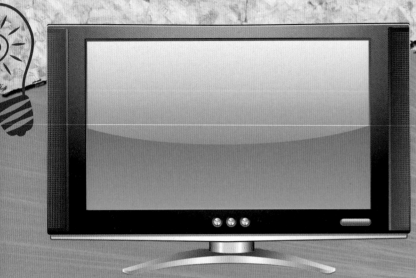

▲ A television works by using **electricity** to make the sound and picture.

Energy is the power that makes things move or work. Cars and buses are powered by chemical energy, such as petrol or diesel fuel. Lights, computers and televisions work by using electrical energy at the flick of a switch.

Energy from the Sun

Plant leaf

Water is taken in from the roots

Oxygen gas is given off

All energy comes originally from the Earth's star, the Sun, which is like an enormous power plant. It sends us energy in sunbeams as heat and light. We turn this into energy that we can use.

Carbon dioxide gas is taken in

◀ Plants take in sunlight and use it with water and carbon dioxide to make their own sugary food. At the same time, they give off oxygen.

Why save energy?

It is important that we try to save as much energy as we can. We are using more coal, oil and gas than ever before, and one day they will all run out.

▲ Coal is a black or brown rock. It is taken from the ground by **mining**, then burned to make electricity.

Did you know?

Coal, oil and natural gas are called fossil fuels. They formed underground millions of years ago from the remains of prehistoric plants and animals.

When we burn fossil fuels in factories and cars, it causes pollution. This makes the air dirty, which damages our environment.

Burning fuels

▲ A car is filled with fuel, such as petrol. This burns inside the car, giving it the power to move.

We burn different forms of oil to power cars, trains, ships and planes. In the home, gas can be burned to cook food and power central heating.

Coal and other fuels are used in **power stations** to make electricity. The fuels are burned, which creates heat. This is then used to boil water, which makes steam. The steam turns the wheel in a machine, which makes electricity.

▲ After making electricity, the hot air is cooled in large towers. The cooling towers give off steam.

You can do it!

Find out how your friends get to school. Do they go by car or bus? Or do they save energy by walking or riding a bike? What about you?

Electric power

Power lines carry electricity from power stations to our neighbourhood. Then cables take it to our homes, schools and businesses. Electricity is instant energy. When we press a switch, there it is!

▲ Power lines are held up by big towers called pylons.

You can do it!

What runs on electricity? Make a chart of the electrical items in the different rooms of your home.

Batteries are small stores of energy. They provide power to make toys, torches, radios and many other electrical items work. Some batteries can be recharged when they are empty and used again.

▲ *These batteries have run out of power. They are put into a recharger, which is plugged into an electrical socket. This charges the batteries with electricity.*

Turn it off!

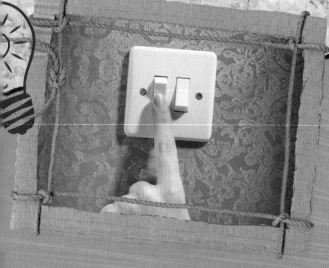

One of the best ways to save energy is to use less electricity at home. It is easy to turn electrical things off when we have finished with them.

▲ *Switching off lights when we are not using them saves a lot of energy.*

Equipment such as televisions often stay on standby when you switch them off with a remote control. They use a small amount of electricity because they are still on. This is a waste of energy.

▶ *Televisions should be switched off properly, instead of using a remote control to put them on standby. Turning off one television saves enough energy every day to power an energy-saving light bulb for six hours.*

TELEVISION

For electrical equipment that needs to be on for a lot of the time, energy can be saved by simply turning it down, rather than off. When it is cold, you could wear an extra jumper and turn the heating down a little.

▶ *Warm clothes can help us to save energy when heating our homes.*

Sun, wind and water

▶ In a wind farm, the blades of turbines turn with the force of the wind. This movement makes electricity.

The energy of sunlight, wind and water can be used to make electricity, too. Solar panels can capture the energy of the Sun. Wind can turn the blades of tall **turbines**. Huge walls across rivers are called dams. They store water to make electricity.

◀ Many calculators are powered by a solar panel — the dark strip at the top. The panel needs to be in the light for the calculator to work.

This kind of energy is called renewable, which means it will not run out. Solar panels are very useful for powering electrical appliances, such as calculators.

You can do it

Hang out washing on a clothes line to see how sunlight and wind dry clothes — without using any electricity!

Muscle power

When you walk or ride a bike, you use muscle power to move. This saves energy because you are not using fuel for a car or bus. It also causes less pollution in the environment.

▶ Riding a bike, walking and running are good exercise.

▶ Food gives us energy. We need energy to make our muscles move.

Our muscles need their own source of energy, just like the rest of our body. All that energy comes from the food that we eat.

You can do it!

Draw a map of your neighbourhood, showing where you can safely walk and ride. Where could there be more paths for pedestrians and cyclists?

Energy in goods

Energy is needed to make things. For example, oil is used to make plastics, paints, tyres and other products. Energy is also used to power the machines that make the goods.

You can do it!

Look on food packets at home or in the supermarket to see where your food comes from. Are the foods local, or have they been brought from far away?

It takes energy to take goods, including food, from one place to another. If we eat food that is grown locally, less energy is used to get the food to our stores.

▼ *We can grow some of our own food, such as fruit and vegetables.*

Wrapping up

▶ A thick layer of **insulation** in the outer walls of a house helps to keep it warm.

It takes energy to heat a building, and energy is wasted if we allow too much heat to escape. We can stop this from happening by using thick layers of material to insulate a house.

◀ *A hat, gloves and coat are insulation for our bodies. They help to keep us warm on a cold day.*

When we go out on a cold day, we wrap up by putting on extra clothes, such as a coat. This stops our bodies from losing too much heat.

Art activities

You can use found objects to make some art-and-craft masterpieces — why buy a brush when you could use a potato? Start making a difference with recycled materials.

Printing a greetings card

what you need

- Thick poster paints
- Card and paper
- Brush
- Scissors
- Printing block (see page 90)

Block prints are a green and easy way of making cool greetings cards. Look at page 90 to find out how to make a printing block, then follow the steps below.

1 Sketch out your ideas for the card design on scrap paper.

2 Now follow the steps on page 90 to make the blocks.

3 Brush the largest printing block with paint. Then press it firmly onto the paper and peel it off to reveal the print beneath.

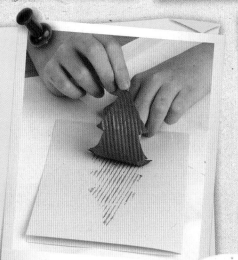

4 When the first colour is dry, do the same with the smaller blocks until your picture is finished. Try not to smudge!

Junk robot

You can make fantastic sculptures out of scrap materials. All you need is some recycled cardboard.

What you need
- A large cardboard box
- Smaller boxes for the robot's head, lower body and feet
- Toilet-paper tubes
- Corrugated card
- PVA glue
- Sticky tape
- Silver paint
- Paintbrush
- Scissors

1 Glue down the top of a large cardboard box. Make a hole in the top and push in a toilet-paper tube. Secure it with sticky tape.

2 Glue on a smaller box to make the lower body. Make two holes underneath and attach tubes for the legs.

3 Tape two toilet-paper tubes together to make each of the robot's arms. Secure them to the robot's body with glue.

4 Cut out eyes and a mouth from corrugated cardboard and glue them to a small cardboard box to make the head.

5 Ask an adult to help you to cut a hole in the bottom of the head and attach it to the robot's neck.

6 Glue on feet made from small cardboard boxes. Paint the robot when the glue is dry.

Collage

what you need

- Colour paper, magazines
- Posterboard or cardboard
- White glue

1 Sketch out a design on cardboard or mount board.

Paper and cardboard are cheap, colourful and easy to cut and paste, which makes them perfect for collage. Keep as many scraps as you can find – you never know when they may come in useful!

2 Tear shapes from the paper or magazines for the design.

3 Arrange the shapes until you are happy with the way they look. Glue them in place on the cardboard.

Cone hats

Re-use old paints, ribbons or glitter to make your own head gear. These hats are great to make and even more fun to wear!

What you need

- Large sheet of cardboard
- Ribbons, sequins, glitter and feathers
- Length of elastic or ribbon
- Glue or sticky tape
- Paint
- Scissors

1 Ask an adult to help you to draw a big circle onto the cardboard. Cut it out, then cut a straight line from the edge of the circle to the exact centre.

2 Overlap the edges to make a cone shape that fits your head, then secure the edges together with glue or tape.

3 Paint your hat and decorate it with ribbons, glitter or paint.

4 Ask an adult to help you make a hole in each side of the hat. Cut a piece of elastic or ribbon and tie it through the holes.

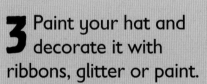

Block prints

What you need
- Styrofoam
- Thick cardboard
- Scissors
- Glue
- Paper
- Paintbrush
- Poster or acrylic paint

You can make a printing block by gluing a foam shape to cardboard or a small block of wood. Printing blocks can be used over and over again.

1 Draw a shape on the styrofoam and ask an adult to help you cut it out.

2 Glue the foam shape to a small block of wood, an empty matchbox or layers of cardboard glued together.

3 Brush the shape with paint, then press it onto paper. You can make several shapes to create a pattern.

'Me' collage

what you need

- Materials for your collage
- Cardboard or posterboard
- PVA glue

Don't let your favourite memories fade away! Recycle items from a holiday or school trip to tell a story about yourself through a collage.

1 Collect items from your holiday or trip. This could be ticket stubs, photos or even coins.

2 Arrange all the items you have collected on a cardboard mount board. Move them around until you are happy with the way they look.

3 Glue down all the bits and pieces to your piece of mount board with PVA glue. Glue a small area at a time.

91

Potato prints

what you need

- Large potato
- Sharp pencil
- Craft knife
- Poster paints
- Paper
- Paintbrush

A potato print is a cross between printing with food and a block.

1 Ask an adult to cut the potato in half. Draw a simple design on the cut surface with a sharp pencil. Try a butterfly, a flower or a star.

2 Ask an adult to cut around the design and remove the excess from the edges so your design sticks out. Brush paint over the surface of the design.

3 Press the painted surface firmly onto paper. Rock the printer gently, so that all parts of the design touch the paper.

Bits and pieces

Scraps and remnants from around the home such as fabric, ribbons, sequins, dried pasta and cocktail sticks look great in collages. You could probably make a collage from the contents of your wastepaper bin!

what you need
- Fluffy feathers
- String
- Cocktail sticks
- Coloured paper
- Beads
- Rice
- PVA glue
- Cardboard
- Scissors

1 Draw the outlines of your picture with a pen, then cut them out. Cut just inside the lines, so that the pen marks don't show, or turn your cut-out shapes the other way round.

2 Arrange the main shapes on the cardboard. When you are happy with the way they look, glue them down.

3 Now add details — a bead for the eye, rice flowers, cocktail sticks and string for a fence, red paper for apples and feathers for a mane and tail.

Using photos

What you need

- Old photographs
- Scissors
- Coloured card
- Old magazines
- PVA glue

A camera can be useful in art. Keep your eyes open for interesting shots, and save photographs from magazines.

1 Want a different home? Take a photo of your house and paint an unusual background to make it look as if you live somewhere different. Look in travel brochures for inspiration.

2 Cut out the house and glue it to a different background. This could be a tropical beach or a snowy mountain.

3 What about adding a friend or a pet to your picture? You could have fun playing with size and proportions, too! In your fantasy picture, objects can be as big or as small as you like.

Material world

What you need
- Cardboard
- Scissors
- PVA glue
- Soft pencil
- Fabrics

It's easy to make fantastic pictures with recycled fabric. You can use anything from an old T-shirt to cotton wool or scraps of lace.

1 First, sketch the outlines of a scene on cardboard in soft pencil. It is best to use cardboard because normal paper might tear.

2 Cut out large background pieces of fabric. You could use blue for the sky, dark green for hills and light green for the fields.

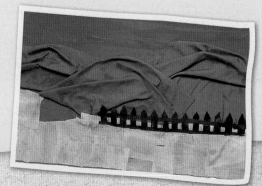

3 Now start adding all the details: maybe a fence, a hedge, trees, animals in the fields, clouds and some flowers... whatever you like!

95

Stencil prints

what you need
- Plain and coloured cardboard
- Thin card for the stencil
- Thick paintbrush
- Poster paints
- Scissors

Cards decorated with stencils are easy to make – and fun to send to your friends!

1 Choose a shape that is symmetrical – the same on both sides.

2 Fold a small square of cardboard in half. Draw half the design at the fold.

3 Carefully cut out your stencil and open it out.

4 Fold a sheet of coloured cardboard in half lengthways.

5 Hold your stencil firmly over the front of the card and dab paint through the stencil with a thick, bristly brush. Let dry.

96

Picture strips

What you need
- Old magazines, or two photos
- Scissors
- Coloured card
- PVA glue

You can use this effect to mix different animals, or alternate an animal with a photo of a celebrity or a landscape.

1 Find two photos or magazine pictures, roughly the same size, and divide them into equal vertical sections 2 cm wide.

2 Cut along the lines to make neat strips.

3 Now glue the first strip from the first picture onto some card, followed by the first strip from the second picture. Keep going, using a strip at a time from each picture, until you've used all the strips.

Painting patterns

Flowers, berries and leaves can be made into works of art. Collect some parts of plants in your garden, then copy their shapes to make a pattern.

1 Look through your collection of leaves, flowers and plants. Make a sketch of some of your favourite shapes.

2 Copy the shapes several times to make a pattern. You could cut each one out and then arrange them.

3 When you have decided on the pattern, glue the pieces in place. Then colour in the pattern using paint. Which colours work best?

Apple prints

What you need

- Poster paints
- Paper
- Short piece of cardboard
- Felt-tip pen

Use your fingertips and thumbs to print these fun animals, then add details with a felt-tip pen.

1 Paint your palm with red paint and press it onto paper.

2 Make a brown stalk by printing with the side of a short piece of cardboard.

3 Press your thumb into green paint to print some leaves.

You can use your fingers to make prints, too

Straw paintings

Recycle a plastic drinking straw and make a *beautiful piece of art.*

1 Add water to some poster or acrylic paint to make the paint runny.

2 Drip a large blob of paint onto your paper with a brush.

3 Gently blow the paint using the straw. The paint will spread across the paper in wiggly lines.

This chick's legs, eyes and beak were added with pencil and orange crayon.

4 Add different colours one by one.

5 Add details with a pencil or crayon or brush to complete your painting.

Still life

What you need

- A bowl of fruit
- Coloured pencils, chalks, crayons or pastels
- Paper

A still life is a drawing or painting of something that does not move, such as flowers in a vase or a bowl of fruit.

1 Take time arranging the fruit in a bowl or on a tabletop until you are happy with the way it looks.

2 Lightly sketch the outline of the bowl first, then draw the fruit. Start with the pieces at the front of the bowl.

3 Draw the pieces of fruit at the back. Only draw the parts of the fruit you can see.

Tiny lines give the orange peel a rough texture

Shading makes the fruit look rounded and three-dimensional

Magazine collage

what you need
- Plenty of old newspapers and magazines
- Cardboard or mount board
- PVA glue
- Scissors

Make a collage from pictures cut or torn from magazines. Choose a theme you find interesting – this one is about food.

1 Find pictures in magazines about your theme. Using safety scissors, cut out as many pictures as you can.

2 Arrange the pictures on your mount board until you like the way they look.

3 Once you are happy, glue the pictures onto the mount board.

Sponge stamps

Sponges are also great for smaller patterns, such as wallpaper for a dolls' house.

1 Draw a simple design on the soft side of the sponge scourer.

2 Ask an adult to cut away the parts around the design using a craft knife.

3 Brush or roll paint over the raised surface and then press the stamp down onto the paper.

103

Scrap collage

what you need
- Thick cardboard
- Materials for the collage (see below)
- Gold or silver spray paint
- PVA glue
- Pencil
- Scissors

Make a picture from scrap materials you may find around your home.

1 Draw the outline of a car on the mount board with a pencil.

This car was made from scrap materials glued to corrugated card. It was then spray-painted silver.

2 Using safety scissors, cut shapes out of paper, cardboard or plastic to fit parts of the car, or arrange items such as buttons, nails or washers in rows.

3 Keep arranging and rearranging the shapes until you are happy with the way they look.

4 Glue down your collage, one small area at a time.

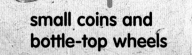

small coins and bottle-top wheels

nuts and bolts

Junk prints

what you need
- Corrugated cardboard
- Empty toilet roll
- Scrunched-up paper bag
- Nails, screws or washers
- Old sponge or cork
- Lego brick or puzzle piece
- Paper

Pieces of junk, such as nails, screws, cardboard or cotton reels, make great prints.

Build up your picture from pieces of junk. Print the junk on rough paper first to see how it looks.

cork

corrugated cardboard

bubble wrap

Lego® brick

Food prints

Print with fruit or vegetables onto scrap fabric to make fun placemats.

1 Set out the food you are going to print with and some dishes of fabric paint. Sketch your design on rough paper first.

2 Ask an adult to help you cut the fabric for the placemats into rectangles, 30 cm x 25 cm. Use pinking shears so the edges don't fray.

3 Dip the food into the paint, or paint the surface of the food with a brush. Press down firmly on the cloth to make the print.

String prints

Make simple printing blocks by gluing string to small pieces of cardboard or wood. The results are amazing!

What you need

- Paper or thin card
- Piece of wood, thick cardboard or a piece of polystyrene for the block
- String
- Poster paints
- Paintbrush
- Glue

1 Paint a blue watery background onto paper or thin card.

2 When the paint is dry, print tall green reeds with the edge of a long piece of cardboard.

3 Glue string to the printing block in a fish shape. Make a large fish block and a smaller one.

4 Glue on string for the fish's scales. Make an eye from string glued in a spiral or a circle of foam.

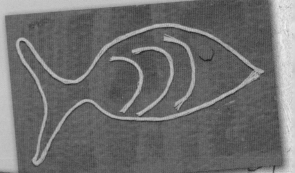

5 Paint the printing block and press onto the background. Paint the block each time you print.

Food collage

Use dried foods, glued to a strong cardboard mount board, to make an imaginative food collage.

1 Glue the black paper onto a strong piece of cardboard to make a mount board.

2 Plan your picture on a piece of white scrap paper first. When you are happy with it, draw it onto the black paper with a white pencil.

3 Choose dried foods for the different parts of your picture.

4 Spread glue thickly over a small part of the picture. Sprinkle small seeds over the glue.

5 Leave the collage flat until the glue has dried completely.

Splitter splatter

What you need
- Old toothbrush
- Paints
- Paper
- Pencil
- Newspaper
- Scissors

Make a lively painting by spattering paint onto paper with an old toothbrush.

1 Draw fish and starfish outlines on a sheet of paper. Turn the paper over and place it face down on some newspaper.

2 Dip a toothbrush in yellow paint, then drag your finger over the bristles to spatter the paint on the paper.

3 Now flick blue and green paint onto a second sheet of paper.

4 When the paint is dry, turn the paper over and cut out the fish and starfish. Arrange them on your sea background and glue them down.

109

Fabric collage

Collages made out of different fabrics are great to look at – and to touch!

1 Plan your picture and draw it lightly on the mount.

Clouds made from scraps of netting and lace

Apples made from scrunched-up scraps of brightly coloured silk fabric

2 Using a pair of scissors, carefully cut the fabric into shapes.

Sheep's soft coats made from flannel

3 Arrange the shapes on the mount until you are happy with the way they look.

4 Glue down the shapes, one small area at a time.

Nature sculpture

Have fun making outdoor sculptures from smooth stones, fallen flowers and leaves, twigs, moss or feathers. You can find all the things you need for free in parks, woods, fields or in your own garden!

Sculpture tips

Natural materials can make great outdoor sculptures. Here are some ideas to start you off:

- Arrange berries in a pattern on moss.
- Overlap fallen leaves in the shape of a circle or a star.
- Arrange flower petals on a stone or rock.
- Make rows of pebbles or shells on the beach.
- If it's been snowing, make a sculpture out of snow.
- If it's been raining, trace lines in mud with a sharp stone or twig, then add a pattern of fallen leaves.

Changing nature

Ask an adult to photograph your nature sculpture. Go back to it the next day and take another photograph to show how it has been changed by wind, rain or animals.

Leaf prints

This project shows you how to make
a printed leaf border for a picture or poem.

what you need
- Selection of clean, dry leaves
- Sugar paper or thin cardboard, 25 cm x 30 cm
- Poster paints
- Brush
- Pencil

1 To make the border, draw a straight line 6 cm in from each side of your sheet of sugar paper or thin card. Ask an adult to cut out the middle section for you.

2 Paint the underside of a leaf and press it onto the frame in one corner.

3 Use the same leaf to make prints in the other corners. Coat the leaf with fresh paint each time.

4 Build up a pattern of leaf shapes in different colours all around the frame. Try beech, oak and sycamore leaves.

Different types of collage

What you need

- Scraps of paper or old magazines
- Cardboard
- Scissors
- PVA glue

Try some different techniques in your collages. What about cutting out lots of small, coloured squares from old magazines and making them into a design, like a Roman mosaic?

You can tear paper into the shapes of animals, flowers and trees.

Experiment with other materials, too, such as buttons, kitchen foil and newspaper. You could also paint bits of paper different colours, tear them up and then use them in your collages. Torn paper creates interesting textures.

You could even make a sculpture out of paper.

113

Printing pictures

Try to think about your prints in a new way – a cabbage leaf print may look just like a cabbage leaf, but it would also make a great tree!

1 Paint the background very quickly, using a wide, soft brush and thin, watered-down paints. Let it dry.

2 Now make lots of tree prints, using cabbage leaves of different sizes.

3 When the 'trees' are dry, cut them out and glue them to the background. Finish the picture by printing the fence, using the edge of a piece of cardboard brushed with brown paint.

Fingerprint rabbit

All you need to create a wildlife masterpiece is some paint and your fingers.

1 Lightly draw the outline of the rabbit in pencil.

2 Now fill in the outline with paint, using your fingers. Let each colour dry before adding the next one.

The grass in this picture was made with a mixture of thumb prints and a twig.

Glossary

Acid rain Rain that has been polluted by waste gases.

Aluminium A non-magnetic, silvery metal.

Biodegradable Something that will rot away.

Bleached Whitened by using chemicals.

Chemical A substance made by mixing other substances together.

Drought A period of very dry weather with no rainfall. The ground dries up.

Electricity An energy supply that we get from wall sockets or batteries.

Environment The world around us.

Fresh water Water that is not salty so we can drink it.

Fuel Something that is burned to provide power.

Incinerator A large furnace (very hot oven) for burning waste.

Insulation Material that stops heat from escaping.

Landfill site A big hole in the ground, where waste is buried.

Litter Small pieces of rubbish on the ground.

Litterbug Someone who drops things on the ground and makes litter.

Local council An organization that governs, or looks after, a neighbourhood, town or district.

Mains Underground pipes used to send water to buildings.

Material A substance used to make things.

Mining Digging rocks, such as coal, from the ground.

Packaging The container that something is put in.

Pollute To damage the environment with harmful substances.

Pollution Damage to the environment caused by harmful substances.

Power station A place where electricity is made.

Pulp A soft, wet mass.

Recycle To make something new out of a thing that has been used before.

Reduce To make the amount of something smaller.

Reservoir A lake where water is stored.

Reuse To use something again.

Sewage Liquid waste matter carried away in drains.

Sewer A large underground pipe that carries dirty water away.

Spring A place where water flows naturally out of the ground.

Steel A strong metal made of iron and carbon.

Turbine A machine that turns to make electricity.

Well A hole dug to get underground water.

Index

Notes for parents and teachers

• It may be difficult for children to appreciate how different the water situation is in developing countries. There are many more facts on the world's water crisis and water stress at www. worldwatercouncil.org*. World Water Day (supported by the United Nations) is on 22 March.

• Consumption of bottled water varies around the world. Average annual consumption per person in litres – Italy 184 litres, France 142 litres, US 91 litres, UK 37 litres, Australia 30 litres and South Africa 2 litres. The world average is 24 litres.

• Walking or cycling to school raise safety issues. Children should be taught that parents and teachers must be aware of what they are doing, and that children must never walk or cycle alone. When cycling, children should wear a safety helmet, reflective clothing and fix lights to their bike.

• Children could learn more about the Sun and what it is – a huge, glowing ball of hot gases, like other stars. The Sun's rays travel at 300,000 kilometres a second and take about eight minutes to reach Earth. Important safety note: never look directly at the Sun. Its bright light could cause permanent damage to your eyes.

• What did people do years ago, before the days of power stations and electricity? Look at how people used to wash and dry clothes, for example, using muscle power and energy from the wind and Sun.

• Go to a supermarket and look at all the things that could be recycled, especially packaging. Discuss why packaging is used (making items, such as food, look attractive). In some countries, shoppers can give packaging straight back to the store at the till point. Come up with other ideas to cut down on packaging.